The Fireside Book

A picture and a poem
for every mood
chosen by
David Hope

Printed and published by
D. C. THOMSON & CO. LTD.
Dundee and London.

TO A SAILING SHIP

PROUD and beautiful ship
    Leaving the peaceful bay,
I would be there with you
    Making your stately way
Round the headland and out to sea,
Into the sky's immensity.

I would be up on deck
    Day after carefree day,
Hearing the waves hiss past,
    Seeing the dolphins play ;
Nightly scanning the brilliant sky,
Watching the stars go wheeling by.

Where the voyage might end
    Would not matter to me,
Were I but one with you
    Out on the lonely sea,
Feeling you thrill to the unseen force
Of winds that sped you upon your course.

Douglas Fraser

IN THE WOODS

THE North winds blow with a promise of snow
    And grey is the autumn sky,
But merry and warm through the woods we go,
  Neddy and Babs and I.

We follow the path through the copses brown
  Where the shadows hide like thieves,
And the sound we hear like a silken gown
  Is Neddy's hoofs in the leaves.

Fluttering down comes a red, red leaf;
  Perhaps from the big beech tree
A fairy is dropping her handkerchief
  To Neddy and Babs and me!

And now we stand while a red-brown head
  Plays hide-and-seek with three—
A squirrel trying to trick old Ned
  And baffle my Babs and me!

But the sun is gone, and the shadows creep,
  And the gold lights flicker and flee;
And Daddies must work and Neddies sleep
  And Babses take their tea.

So we wave one arm to the darkening firs,
  And one to the sunset sky,
And home we go—my hand in hers—
  Neddy, and Babs and I.

Will H. Ogilvie

I'D LIKE TO KNOW

THE things that pine trees whisper
　In the still and dead of night,
The ageless tune that wild geese chant,
　Through the long hours of flight.

I'd like to know what waters say,
　Flowing toward the sea,
I'm sure they speak of quiet springs,
　Back where they used to be —

Of sloping banks where cowslips bloom
　And trees whose feet are pressed
Against the heart of Mother Earth,
　Where all things come to rest.

I'd like to hear the ageless song
　That lonely mountains know,
When winter crowns their ancient peaks
　With diadems of snow.

The language of the quiet beasts,
　Must be a friendly thing,
When something deep within their breasts,
　Is telling them of spring.

For Earth and all that dwells therein
　Are part and parcel to
The spark of that eternal life,
　That beats inside of you.

Edna Jacques

THE UNIVERSAL AUNT

THERE was a hen at Tipperty
    That hatched a brood o' ducks,
And led them tae the waterside
    Wi' prood maternal clucks.

And when the fluffy little teds
    Were launched upo' the dam,
A ferly see, in stappit she,
    An' wided whaur they swam.

Her scaly legs grew white as milk,
    Weet were her feather breeks,
An' in she raxed her horny neb
    Whan doon dabbed yellow beaks.

She herded a' her paiddlin' brood
    Frae cressy bank tae bank,
An' wided but an' wided ben
    On carefu', balanced shank.

Ferly — wonder. Stappit — stepped.
Raxed — reached. But and ben — here and there.
Skeely — clever.

" Noo heaven uphaud ye, skeely hen,
    Ye're daft, ye love-a-duck!''
Her beady e'e she winked at me,
    An' " Cluck,'' she said, juist " Cluck!''

Helen B. Cruickshank

DUSKY

BLACK, glossy, beautiful,
    my spaniel darts
madly in wakened woods—
scrambles in pebbly pools,
exults in heather;
dashes in danger—leaps
over the walls—a cat
the end-all of his mind,
traffic-erased . . .

Caught in a current, Dusky's energy
and iron resolution
saved his life—
and once he swallowed
broken glass—unscathed.

Yet with his wildness goes
the gentleness
of cocker hearts.
At night his basket holds
a quiet dog,
hazed-over and content—
our cyclone then becomes
a soft black cloud.

May C. Jenkins

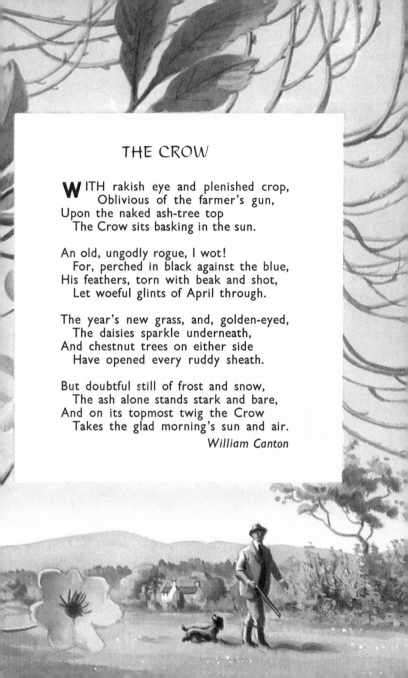

THE CROW

WITH rakish eye and plenished crop,
   Oblivious of the farmer's gun,
Upon the naked ash-tree top
  The Crow sits basking in the sun.

An old, ungodly rogue, I wot!
  For, perched in black against the blue,
His feathers, torn with beak and shot,
  Let woeful glints of April through.

The year's new grass, and, golden-eyed,
  The daisies sparkle underneath,
And chestnut trees on either side
  Have opened every ruddy sheath.

But doubtful still of frost and snow,
  The ash alone stands stark and bare,
And on its topmost twig the Crow
  Takes the glad morning's sun and air.

William Canton

POLITICS

YOU say a thousand things
    persuasively.
And with strange passion hotly I agree
And praise your zest,
And then
A blackbird sings
On April lilac, or fieldfaring men,
Ghost-like, with loaded wain,
Come down the twilit lane
To rest;
And what is all your argument to me?

Oh, yes—I know, I know.
It must be so—
You must devise
Your myriad politics.
For we are little wise,
And must be led and marshalled; lest we keep
Too fast a sleep
Far from the central world's realities.
Yes, we must heed—
For surely you reveal
Life's very heart: surely, with flaming zeal
You search our folly and our secret needs
And surely it is wrong
To count my blackbird's song,
My cones of lilac, and my wagon team
More than a world of dream.
But still
A voice calls from the hill.
I must away
I cannot hear your argument today.

John Drinkwater

WALKING ON SUNDAY

(Beside the Cherwell)

BESIDE the stream where blackbirds talk,
　　The old and young, and lovers walk.
Here, chestnuts rear their candled heads;
There, willows spring from marshy beds:
The air is sweet with rain-washed may,
Both red and white, along the way.
And hark! I hear the splash of pole
Like plopping of a water-vole,
As drifting slow, appears in sight,
A cushioned punt—with youth in white,
Who wields the pole ; his eyes admire
The girl he steers with hair afire
Or so it seems—so flaming red
The sun-kissed curls that cap her head.
A dog sniffs here—a child trots there—
The lady's-lace froths everywhere
Along the banks that verge the stream;
And on the bridge where waters cream,
A youngster leans to watch them race
With rapt absorption on his face.
And you are with me as I walk;
Although alone, I hear you talk
Like once you did; I loved you so
When we strolled here—ah, long ago!

Violet Bowen

BLUE BLOOD

DELICATELY groomed and chic
    I am a very high-born peke!
Round my eyes and pink my tongue—
Graces all the bards have sung.
Emperors loved my winning way
Ages back in old Cathay.
At court we lived in pampered ease
Sheltered from the slightest breeze.
Transported to these Western parts
We found a way to ladies' hearts—
Though Western gents prefer, I fear,
Coarser beasts that hunt the deer.
Let such breeds by action score,
Our blood demands of us no more
Than demonstrate, by bearing chic,
How elegant the high-born peke!

David Hope

The little " Lion Dog " of China, the aristocratic and much revered lap-dog of the Imperial Court, the Pekingese came to Britain in 1860. Five puppies were found by the Dragoon Guards while storming the Summer Palace in Peking. They were brought to England and one of them became Queen Victoria's pet " Looty."

PERHAPS ITS YOU!

THE busy rooks are building
   By the stream in Cushendall,
The primroses are blooming
   Up at Ess-na-Laragh fall,
The hills are crowned with whin-gold
   And there's lark-song in the blue,
But I feel there's something wanting
   And—perhaps it's you!

The woods are filled with music
  In the vale of Cushendun,
The little white-washed cottage
  Lies a-gleaming in the sun,
There are thrushes in the garden
  And I think they're courting, too,
But I feel there's something wanting
  And—perhaps it's you!

May Morton

A MORNING IN SUMMER

" I LOVE you so—you *know* I do!" you said.
   Stillness was round us and the air serene.
With lifting heart I saw the morning sky,
   The dreaming trees that never were so green.

Oh, love me always, darling, just as much,
   And be the glad companion of my ways,
And take my love and joy and endless trust,
   To thread with gold the fair or flinty days.

Your love as bright and warm as now it is,
   Your gentle dreams to share the sweet years
      through—
What more to ask?—to hear you say again—
   " I love you, dear. You know, you *know* I do."

May C. Jenkins

CLYDESDALES

A Vanishing Picture

A FIELD is ploughed. The long, straight furrows
      gleam,
Ruled by a perfect partnership of three:
The ploughman urging on his willing team,
The two great horses in their majesty.

At hedge-side, see their tossings of the head
Until the plough is turned and set on course;
A stamp, a heave, then off with measured tread,
The twin embodiments of vital force.

Could any sight be finer? There they go
With swooping seagulls screaming in their wake,
Steady and purposeful, as, row by row,
New furrows mark the progress that they make.

Patient and docile giants of the farm,
How well you keep your strength for useful ends.
If men—so clever—did as little harm,
All might be brothers yet, as you are friends.

Douglas Fraser

HOMESPUN

I MET a man in Harris tweed
  As I went down the Strand;
I turned and followed like a dog
That breath of hill and sea and bog
That clung about the crotal brown.
And suddenly, in London Town
I heard again the Gaelic speech,
The scrunch of keel on shingly beach;
The traffic's never-ending roar
Came plangent from a shining shore;
I saw the little lochs where lie
The lilies, white as ivory;
And tumbling down the rocky hills
Came scores of little foaming rills.

I saw the crofter bait his line,
The children herding yellow kine,
The barefoot woman with her creel,
The washing-pot, the spinning-wheel,
The mounds thrown up by patient toil
To coax the corn from barren soil.

With buoyant step I went along
Whistling a Hebridean song
That Ian Og of Taransay
Sang to me one enchanted day.
I was a man renewed indeed
Because I smelt that Harris tweed
As I went down the Strand.

Helen B. Cruickshank

LONGINGS

HERE, where the warmer breezes blow,
   Along the hedges, row on row,
     Blossoms the dog-rose fair:
But yonder through the distant haze,
The heather blooms upon the braes—
     And oh that I were there!

Sweetly I hear the skylark fill
With its full-throated mellow trill,
     The quiet evening air:
But where the broad haughs fallow lie
I think I hear the peesweep cry
     And oh that I were there!

Calm flows the river to the shore,
Smooth where her placid reaches o'er,
     Knee-deep the anglers fare:
But still I see the hill-streams brown,
Where callants burn the water* down—
     And oh that I were there!

And oh that I were there again
Where the hills lift from the green glen
     And the strong men till the loam.
My ears yearn for their soft speech,
For their firm grip my hands reach—
     My heart, my heart is home!

                    Ian Chalmers

* *Burn the water—attract salmon by lantern light.*

A CHILD NEEDS A GRANDMA

A CHILD needs a grandma to spoil him a bit.
   Someone with time on their hands who will
   sit
On an old-fashioned rocker that shivers and squeaks,
   And listen to words that a little boy speaks.

Someone who knows how a gingerbread man
   All crumbly and fragrant and warm from the pan
Can comfort a fellow who feels a bit blue,
   And nothing just right seems to happen to you.

A child needs a grandma to teach him the words,
   That run like a hymn in the song of the birds,
Someone who knows where the orioles go,
   When the garden is covered with inches of snow.

And only a grandma remembers to say
   " Now be a good boy " as she tucks him away,
Under the covers and pats them down tight,
   For little boys sometimes get scared in the night.

A child needs the comforting knowledge of love,
   Steady and sure as the stars up above,
To carry him safely through sunshine and tears,
   A light in the darkness . . . a stay through the
    years.

A child needs a grandma to nod in her chair,
And give him her blessing by just being there.

Edna Jaques

SEPTEMBER

BE my theme, beloved September,
  'Tis the time for quiet thought;
When the fields, white unto harvest,
  Show what God and man hath wrought;
'Tis the month for calm reflection,
  When the day is on the wane;
And a halo of remembrance
  Circles round the golden grain.

At the noontide in September,
  Happy fields are all astir,
And the atmosphere is vibrant
  With the busy reaper's whirr;
Soon the corn sheaves will be lifted,
  And the stooks will proudly stand,
Lending dignity and beauty
  To a fair and pleasant land.

In the evenings of September,
  When the quiet dews descend,
O we love the hallowed gloaming
  When the light and darkness blend;
Then the swain becomes expansive,
  And less shy the maiden's glance;
Ah, full many a heart is plighted
  At the happy harvest dance!

So my theme's beloved September—
  'Tis the month of all the year
Which, through all life's varied changes,
  Most delightful doth appear;
Though I love the springtime's promise,
  And the charms of summer own,
Yet the autumn brings fulfilment—
  And September is its crown.

George Stephen

BY THE SEA

CHIMING a dream by the way
  With ocean's rapture and roar,
I met a maiden today
  Walking alone on the shore.
Walking in maiden wise,
  Modest and kind and fair,
The freshness of spring in her eyes
  And the fulness of spring in her hair.

Cloud-shadow and scudding sun-burst
  Were swift on the floor of the sea,
And a mad wind was romping its worst,
  But what was their magic to me?
What the charm of the midsummer skies?
  I only saw she was there,
A dream of the sea in her eyes
  And the kiss of the sea in her hair.

I watched her vanish in space ;
  She came where I walked no more ;
But something had passed of her grace
  To the spell of the wave and the shore ;
And now, as the glad stars rise,
  She comes to me rosy and rare,
The delight of the wind in her eyes
  And the hand of the wind in her hair.

                    W. E. Henley

NEST EGGS

BIRDS all the sunny day
  Flutter and quarrel
Here in the arbour-like
  Tent of the laurel.

Here in the fork
  The brown nest is seated;
Four little blue eggs
  The mother keeps heated.

While we stand watching her,
  Staring like gabies,
Safe in each egg are the
  Birds' little babies.

Soon the frail eggs they shall
  Chip, and upspringing
Make all the April woods
  Merry with singing.

Younger than we are,
  O children, and frailer,
Soon in blue air they'll be.
  Singer and sailor.

We, so much older,
  Taller and stronger,
We shall look down on the
Birdies no longer.

They shall go flying
With musical speeches
High overhead in the
  Tops of the beeches.

In spite of our wisdom
  And sensible talking,
We on our feet must go
  Plodding and walking.

                    R. L. Stevenson.

NICHOLAS NYE

THISTLE and darnel and dock grew there,
  And a bush, in the corner, of may.
On the orchard wall I used to sprawl
  In the blazing heat of the day;
Half-asleep and half-awake,
  While the birds went twittering by,
And nobody there my lone to share
  But Nicholas Nye.

Alone with his shadow he'd drowse in the meadow,
  Lazily swinging his tail,
At the break of day he used to bray—
  Not much too hearty and hale;
But a wonderful gumption was under his skin,
  And a clear calm light in his eye,
And once in a while: he'd smile . . .
  Would Nicholas Nye.

Seem to be smiling at me, he would,
  From his bush in the corner, of may—
Bony and ownerless, widowed and worn,
  Knobble-kneed, lonely and grey;
And over the grass would seem to pass
  'Neath the deep dark blue of the sky,
Something much better than words between me
  And Nicholas Nye.

But dusk would come in the apple boughs,
  The green of the glow-worm shine,
The birds in nest would crouch to rest,
  And home I'd trudge to mine;
And there, in the moonlight, dark with dew,
  Asking not wherefore nor why,
Would brood like a ghost, and as still as a post,
  Old Nicholas Nye.

                    Walter de la Mare

A SONG OF THE ROAD

THE gauger walked with willing foot,
    And aye the gauger played the flute;
And what should Master Gauger play
But *Over the hills and far away?*

When'er I buckle on my pack
And foot it gaily in the track,
O pleasant gauger, long since dead,
I hear you fluting on ahead.

You go with me the self-same way—
The self-same air for me you play;
For I do think and so do you
It is the tune to travel to.

For who would gravely set his face
To go to this or t'other place?
There's nothing under heav'n so blue
That's fairly worth the travelling to.

On every hand the roads begin,
And people walk with zeal therein;
But wheresoe'er the highways tend,
Be sure there's nothing at the end.

Then follow you, wherever hie
The travelling mountains of the sky.
Or let the streams in civil mode
Direct your choice upon a road;

For one and all, or high or low,
Will lead you where you wish to go;
And one and all go night and day
Over the hills and far away

R. L. Stevenson

THINGS THAT MATTER

GIVE me a good digestion, Lord,
 And also something to digest;
Give me a healthy body, Lord
 With sense to keep it at its best;
Give me a healthy mind, good Lord,
 To keep the good and pure in sight,
Which, seeing sin, is not appalled
 But finds a way to set it right;
Give me a mind that is not bored,
 That does not whimper, whine, or sigh;
Don't let me worry overmuch
 About a fussy thing called I.
Give me a sense of humour, Lord,
 Give me the grace to see a joke,
To get some happiness from life
 And pass it on to other folk.

Prayer found in Chester Cathedral

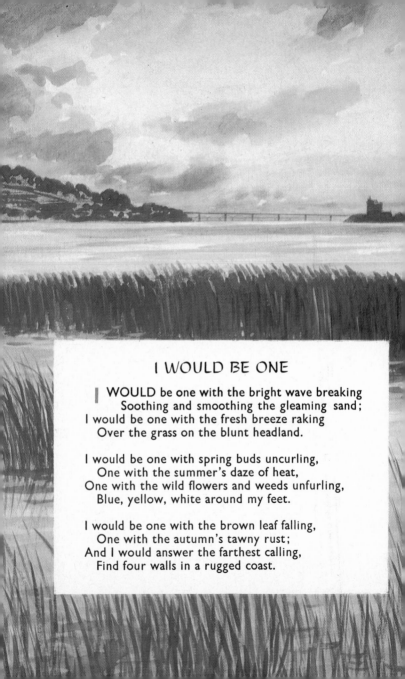

I WOULD BE ONE

I WOULD be one with the bright wave breaking
   Soothing and smoothing the gleaming sand;
I would be one with the fresh breeze raking
  Over the grass on the blunt headland.

I would be one with spring buds uncurling,
  One with the summer's daze of heat,
One with the wild flowers and weeds unfurling,
  Blue, yellow, white around my feet.

I would be one with the brown leaf falling,
  One with the autumn's tawny rust;
And I would answer the farthest calling,
  Find four walls in a rugged coast.

In winter, too, with the strong gales pouring
    Wind and rain on the island's hull,
I would be one with the dark tide snoring,
    One with kittiwake, petrel, gull.

In every season I could find haven,
    Even when thundering tempests roar,
Here on the island's earthly heaven;
    One with the elements evermore.

R. L. Cook

FIRELIGHT

NOW it is evening: draw the curtain
      close,
   The mist creeps round us from the grey hillside;
Here in the firelight let us think of those
   Far friends most with us in this eventide.

Do they at evening, in the camp-fire's glow,
   Pine for green fields seen from the cottage door,
Or sigh for all the country sights they know—
   How Autumn's beech leaves strew the valley's
      floor,

How the last apple on the topmost bough
   Glistens and reddens in the westering sun,
And hungry birds follow the heavy plough,
   And every chimney smokes with fires begun ?

Pile on the logs, among the rafters dark
   Send dancing shadows; here, at England's core,
We'll keep a welcome warm till they embark
   And knock with eager hands upon the door.

Cecil Roberts

ROBIN IN THE WINTER ORCHARD

ROBIN'S silver whistle
   Sounds sweetly in the air
As though he hasn't noticed
   That all the trees are bare;
That where the leaves once hid him
   And all the apples shone,
Spread skeletons of branches
   With all the baubles gone;
He perches on a twiglet
   So berry-bright and spry
In contrast with the snow-clouds
   That bruise the wintry sky;
With ice upon the rain-butts
   And puddles glazed like glass,
And all the worms and insects
   Deep-frozen in the grass,
Yet, up aloft sits robin
   Bedight in scarlet vest,
An undismayed wee fellow
   And very welcome guest.

Violet Bowen

CELTIC CROSS

THREE symbols here I send in one,
   A Celtic Cross with a cairngorm stone.

The mystic Cross in the forefront glows;
Its depth and wonder no man knows.

The Circle of Prayer like a shining road
Links friend with friend and all with God.

The stone was polished and cut to fit,
Till the light shone through, transforming it.

As the rugged soul, by sin laid bare,
Is chiselled in love, and comes out fair.

So the love of God and the faith of Man
Combine to further the heavenly plan.

And in this Cross I read the sign
That our love is blessed in the Love Divine.

Three symbols, Dear, I send in one,
A Celtic Cross with a cairngorm stone.

Alison Clare

LOVE OLD AND NEW

AND were they not the happy days
 When love and I were young,
When earth was robed in heavenly light,
 And all creation sung ?
When gazing in my true love's face,
 Through greenwood alleys lone,
I guessed the secrets of her heart,
 By whispers of mine own.

And are they not the happy days
 When love and I are old,
And silver evening has replaced
 A morn and noon of gold ?
Love stood alone mid youthful joy,
 But now by sorrow tried,
It sits and calmly looks to heaven
 With angels at its side.

Charles Mackay

ONE WAY OF FRIENDSHIP

WHEN a friend performs a favour,
It would have a sweeter savour
If he did it in the way that you desired.
He would make you more his debtor,
If he did not know, far better
Than the person who requires it, what's required.

He contrives with zeal officious,
Plans more safe and expeditious
  Than the method you would like to see employed;
And you find, when all is ended,
He has missed what you intended,
  And has done what you were anxious to avoid.

If you thank him somewhat coldly,
He will turn and tell you boldly
  That ingratitude becomes you very ill.
Should you wish again to use him,
Will it please you to excuse him?
  And you answer with conviction that it will.

R. F. Murray

MOONLIT APPLES

AT the top of the house the apples are laid in
    rows,
And the skylight lets the moonlight in, and those
Apples are deep-sea apples of green. There goes
    A cloud on the moon in the autumn night.

A mouse in the wainscot scratches, and scratches,
    and then
There is no sound at the top of the house of men
Or mice; and the cloud is blown, and the moon
    again
    Dapples the apples with deep-sea light.

They are lying in rows there, under the gloomy
    beams;
On the sagging floor; they gather the silver streams
Out of the moon, those moonlit apples of dreams,
    And quiet is the steep stair under.

In the corridors under there is nothing but sleep.
And stiller than ever on orchard boughs they keep
Tryst with the moon, and deep is the silence, deep
    On moon-washed apples of wonder.

John Drinkwater

SMALL CREATURES

SMALL creatures go
    Their secret ways
In woods and fields and ditches;
We little know
How pass their days
Or guess the teeming riches
Concealed about
A patch of heath,
A marsh, a dune, a clearing,
Some peeping out,
Some safe beneath,
Some glimpsed while disappearing.
While rabbits hop
And weasels glide
And mice dart here and yonder,
Frogs leap and flop,
Snails stretch and slide
And hedgehogs like to wander.
Men fight a foe,
Pursue a craze
Or plan some new invention:
Small creatures go
Their secret ways
And pay us scant attention.

Douglas Fraser

DOWN TO THE SHORE

DOWN to the shore where the waves are
    breaking
    Will you come out with me?
Watching the bents in the salt gusts shaking ;
    Viewing the restless sea ;

Noting the seaweed rising, falling ;
    Dodging the high-tossed spray ;
Hearing the redshanks' plaintive calling
    Out in the open bay ;

Watching the water, flung on ledges
    Under the sea's attack,
Creaming over their rocky edges
    As each spent wave falls back ;

Seeing the surf slide up the shingle
    As breakers pound the shore ;
Hearing a score of sounds that mingle
    Into a steady roar ;

Feeling the wind upon our faces ;
    Tasting the salt sea-spray ;
Knowing that out in the open spaces
    Cobwebs are swept away ;

Down to the shore where the waves are breaking,
    Viewing the restless sea,
Books and papers and fire forsaking,
    Will you come out with me?

Douglas Fraser

ONE-MAN BAND

HE steps with a swing and a swagger
　　Where traffic rolls loudly along,
And rushing folk halt in their hurrying
　　To savour the ring of his song.

His sticks beat their tattoo so merry
　　And weave their blithe rings bonnet-high,
His knees knock the cymbals a-clatter
　　His shrill whistles pierce the night sky.

The winds catch the lilt of his music,
　　The tails of his Balmoral wave,
And tired feet start with new vigour
　　As out pipes old "Scotland the Brave."

To bands at the castle or gardens,
　　The plaudits of critics are thrown,
But I lift my hat to the minstrel,
　　The man with a song of his own.

William Landles

MY LADDIE

I WILL knit him a foam-white jersey,
  Soft as the breast of the mew;
Or, if he prefers, he
  May have it of deep-sea blue.

I will knit him stockings of crimson
  Soft as the fall of flowers,
Of the colour that dims on
  The islands in evening hours.

And I will knit him a bonnet
  Soft as the breast of the dove,
With tassel-bobs on it—
  Oh, my laddie, my love!

Hamish McLaren

I DREAM OF A PLACE

I DREAM of a place where I long to live always:
   Green hills, shallow sand dunes, and nearing
   the sea;

The house is of stone; there are twelve lattice
   windows,
And a door, with a keyhole—though lost is the key.

Thick-thatched is the roof; it has low, white-
   washed chimneys,
Where doves preen their wings, and coo, *Please,
   love: love me!*

There martins are flitting; the sun shines; the
   moon shines;
Drifts of bright flowers are adrone with the bee;

And a wonderful music of bird-song at daybreak
Wells up from the bosom of every tree.

A brook of clear water encircles the garden,
With kingcups, and cress and the white *fleur de lys*—

Moorhens and dabchicks; the wild duck at evening
Wing away to the sun, in the shape of a V;

And the night shows the stars, shining in at the
    windows,
Brings nearer the faraway sigh of the sea.

Oh, the quiet, the green of the grass, the grey
    willows,
The light, and the shine, and the air sweet and free!

That dream of a place where I long to live always:
Low hills, shallow sand dunes—at peace there to be!

Walter de la Mare

THE SHEPHERD

KEEN blows the wind over Braidhope, but close
    is my warm plaid wound;
It's a gey bit step on the hirsel from the haugh to
    the hill-top ground,
But there's lift in the heart of the heather, there's
    wine in the wind from the sea,
And up o'er the shoulder of Braidhope — light
    tramping for Laddie and me.

Bord'ring the burn with their silver the swords of
    the fairies are bright;
Hiding the grips and the hollows the snow-wreaths
    lie crested and white;
Near all of the flock is beneath us laid close in the
    lap of the lee,
But there's aye a few wandering wastrels make
    labour for Laddie and me.

The shadows sweep up from the valley, the dark
    hirples down from the hill;
At the bend of the glen is a cottage and a candle
    burns bright on the sill;
Now the snowflakes may break from the purple,
    the snow-clouds roll up from the sea,
For the ewes are all bonnily bielded* and home
    beckons Laddie and me.

There are roads that are smoother to travel, I grant
    you, but go where I will
There is never a pathway that calls me like this that
    leads over the hill,
When the west wind comes up from the Solway
    in the sleety chain mail of the sea
To trample the bracken on Braidhope and wrestle
    with Laddie and me.

Will H. Ogilvie

* sheltered

A LITTLE GIRL COMES TO VISIT

OLD house, you need no longer be so staid.
    Smile now, for soon upon your silent stairs,
Quick feet will sound again and chubby legs
    Will dangle from your tall, plush-cushioned
        chairs.

A laughing, curl-framed face will gayly tint
    Time-misted mirrors, and a little head
Will dimple pillows, stiffly smooth; a sweet,
    Small body warm the chill four-poster bed.

Old garden, standing quiet, laugh aloud!
    With butterflies, along your paths she'll run,
Her skirts as perky as your hollyhocks,
    Her hair a-shimmer at the touch of sun!

Perennials, whose certain loveliness
    Is beauty grown familiar to our eyes,
Lift up your heads, phlox, larkspur, pinks,
    One comes who will behold you with surprise!

Old house, old garden now give welcome, sing
To her who comes upon you, wondering!

                                    Violet Alleyn Storey

BY AN OLD BRIDGE

BENEATH the ancient moss-clad bridge
    The sullen waters flow,
While ferns and reedy grasses bend
  In rhythm, as they go
Towards the open northern sea
  Where wind-whipp'd waves roll high.
And overhead, and overcast,
  A wintry, leaden sky.

A shaft of gold transforms the view,
  Breaks thro' from out the grey,
And lends a brief enchantment to
  A North-East winter's day.

Janet Coutts

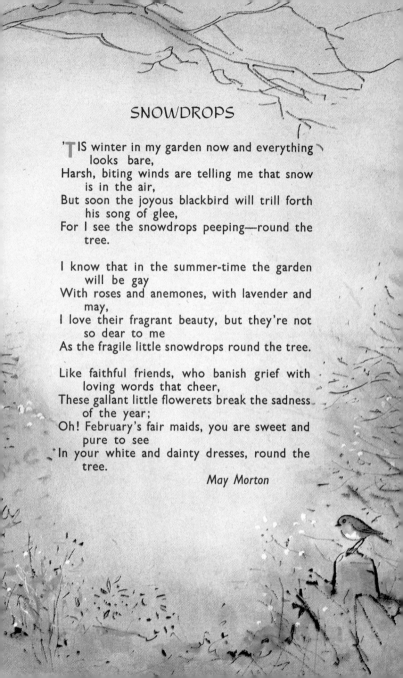

SNOWDROPS

'TIS winter in my garden now and everything
    looks bare,
Harsh, biting winds are telling me that snow
    is in the air,
But soon the joyous blackbird will trill forth
    his song of glee,
For I see the snowdrops peeping—round the
    tree.

I know that in the summer-time the garden
    will be gay
With roses and anemones, with lavender and
    may,
I love their fragrant beauty, but they're not
    so dear to me
As the fragile little snowdrops round the tree.

Like faithful friends, who banish grief with
    loving words that cheer,
These gallant little flowerets break the sadness
    of the year;
Oh! February's fair maids, you are sweet and
    pure to see
In your white and dainty dresses, round the
    tree.

May Morton

HOME

HOME is a distant glimmer,
  A faint but welcome sight
Across the frozen furrows
  In fading winter light.

Home is a lamplit window
  Casting a golden glow
Over an empty garden
  And the cold, blue sheen of snow.

Home is a cheerful fireplace
  In a room that's warm and snug,
Two easy chairs beside it,
  The dog asleep on the rug.

Home is two hearts united,
  At ease and well prepared
To face life's every challenge
  With every burden shared.

Douglas Fraser

BUTTERCUPS

BUTTER'S cheap in fairyland, there's cups of it
        and cups of it,
   Along the grassy tablecloth as far as can be seen;
Butter's cheap in fairyland, there's not a bee but
        sups of it,
   And no one in the meadow even mentions mar-
        garine.

Butter's cheap in fairyland, I saw a baby buying it,
   Her pinafore was full of it and both her buffy
        hands:
A smile was all the price she paid—a smile and no
        denying it,
   This clever little market wife that knows her
        meadowland.

Butter's cheap in fairyland, but not for every one
        of us:
   The heart must be as pure as snow, the soul be
        bright and clean:
Without the smile that knows no guile, the fairies
        will have none of us,
   And we shall find within the cups, not even mar-
        garine.

                              Will H. Ogilvie

MURLOUGH BAY

IF I live to be a hundred,
   Sure I'll not forget the day
We were roamin' on the mountain
   When we came on Murlough Bay,
With the white strand that's in it,
   And the corner where we lay
Tellin' how we'd climb the headland,
   Though it looked so tall and gray,
And we'd swim across to Scotland
   For it wasn't far away!
(And indeed we really meant to
   When we came some other day).

Och! the rocks were just like jewels
    With the sunshine and the spray,
And the grass was green with fairies
    (Though it wouldn't do to say);
There are hills all over Antrim
    Where they go at night to play,
But it's only down in Murlough
    That you'd see them through the day!

May Morton

TRANQUILLITY

I WILL give thanks to God for peaceful things,
  For tranquil nights, star-sprinkled — lonely
    trees
And grass that quivers in the summer breeze,
For sunlight sparkling on a seagull's wings.

For moonbeams sleeping on a quiet lake,
  For the long hush after the noise of day,
  The little lapping waves, the shining spray,
The candid beauty of the world awake.

For old-world gardens, sunk in cloudy mists,
  And secrets that the dull world never hears,
  For tenderness and laughter, close on tears,
For all the soundless music that exists.

For a child's look of wondering thoughtfulness,
  For gentle words of comfort, that reveal
  To wounded souls that peace alone may heal —
Through broken dreams, the way to happiness.

               May C. Jenkins

FIRST DAY AT SCHOOL

NEGLECTED toys are limp and strange,
    And empty stairs reach silent rooms—
The five-year-old has gone to school.

Now in the blank untrampled house
His mother stands. A knife of light
Pierces the room . . . Is he in tears ?
Stunned by the strangeness, lost ?
Or wondering and glad in his new life ?

The crawling hours go numbly past.
Lunch-time at last ! She dashes out—
Too early, she has reached the gates . . .

Philip comes tumbling out of school—
His beaming face, his shining eyes
Reveal a morning's happiness
And brings his mother vivid joy—
At once, her loneliness is eased.

May C. Jenkins

HOMECOMING

CLIFFS breaking through the haze,
  And a narrowing sea,
Soon will my eager gaze
  Have sight of thee,

England, the lovelier now
  For absence long,
Soon shall I see your brow,
  Hear a lark's song.

Heart, curb your beating—there
  Channel cliffs glow,
Eddystone, Plymouth, where
  Drake mounts the Hoe!

Red of the Devon loam,
  Green of the hills,
April! and I am home,
  God, my heart thrills!

Far have I travelled and
  Great beauty seen,
But oh, out of England
  Is anywhere green?

Thankful and thankful again
  As never before,
One of the Englishmen
  Comes to his shore!

Cecil Roberts

I LIKE A KID THAT WHISTLES

I LIKE a kid that whistles,
　　When I hear his merry note,
I feel a sort of answering song
　　Swelling in my own throat,
As if I too must share the joy,
Of my nice mannered paper boy.

I like to hear a woman sing
　　When polishing her floors,
Getting a meal or doing up
　　The common household chores,
For laughter has a happy tone,
And a good flavour all its own.

I like a man who smiles and sings,
　　And tells a kindly joke,
Whose workshop is a meeting place,
　　For half the country folk,
Who find in his warm-hearted laugh
Their little troubles cut in half.

For laughter lays a tender spell,
　　On all who know her ways,
Like a beloved guest who brings
　　A blessing where she stays,
Whistles and laughter . . . songs and mirth,
Are among the sweetest things of earth.

Edna Jaques

IN NATURE'S GARDEN

WE wandered to the pine forest
    That skirts the ocean foam
The lightest wind was in its nest,
  The tempest in its home;
The whispering waves were half-asleep,
  The clouds were gone to play,
And on the bosom of the deep
  The smile of Heaven lay;
It seemed as if the hour were one
  Sent from beyond the skies,
Which scattered from above the sun
  A light of Paradise.

P. B. Shelley

SPRING SALMON

IT'S oh, but I'm dreaming
　　Of grey water streaming,
Great rivers that go gleaming
　　Where brown the heather blows,
Ere May's southern graces
Rub out the last white traces
From high and mountain places
　　Of stubborn, storm-packed snows!

The chill wind that searches
The low-lying birches,
The old red grouse that perches
　　And swaggers in the sun ;
I'm fain for its blowing,
I'm restless for his crowing,
And it's I that would be going
　　Where the spring salmon run!

And oh, were they bulking
Bright silver, or sulking —
In the snow-broth a-skulking,
　　I would care not at all,
I'd hear the falls ringing,
I'd see the pine-tops swinging
In a wind that's filled with singing
　　When the green plover call!

Patrick R. Chalmers

COUNTRY THOUGHTS

WHEN I walk by Buckingham Palace,
　　Where the Queen works hard all day,
Does she long to live in a cottage, I wonder,
And dream the hours away,
And never see a minister but only make decrees
Concerning new asparagus beds
And planting cherry trees?

When I walk by the Houses of Parliament
Where the grey old Thames sweeps by,
Does the Speaker forget to listen, I wonder,
And dream in his Chair, and sigh
To hear the quacking of the geese around the old
　　barn door,
Forgetting all the garrulous flock
That fills the Commons floor?

When I walk by Hyde Park Corner,
And the trees of Rotten Row,
Guardsmen in red coats stand like tulips,
And quick the nursemaids grow,
And little tots all potted out, in prams well-bedded
　　down,
Lift flowery faces, starry-eyed,
To brighten London Town.

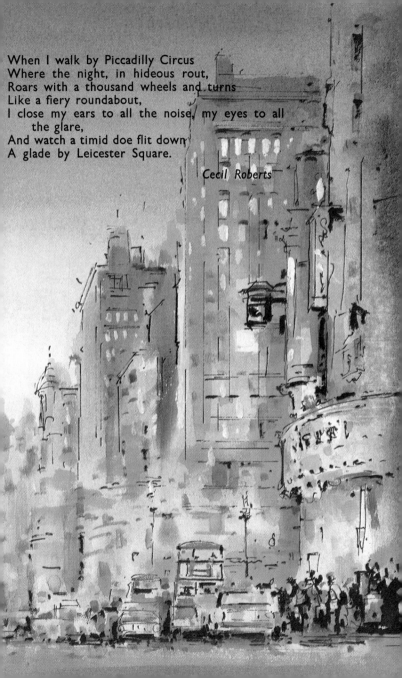

When I walk by Piccadilly Circus
Where the night, in hideous rout,
Roars with a thousand wheels and turns
Like a fiery roundabout,
I close my ears to all the noise, my eyes to all
  the glare,
And watch a timid doe flit down
A glade by Leicester Square.

Cecil Roberts

A WESTMORLAND WALL

MOSS-GROWN and weathered green and
    brown:
  And one man built it, so they say—
For a bet or just for pleasure
  Between dawn and sunset in one day.

He scorned the use of mortar and brick
  He dug and quarried every stone,
Refused all help and built his wall
  In one day, working all alone.

Six feet high and a mile in length,
  Straight as a sapling over the fell,
Dividing nothing, it yet stands
  A monument to work done well.

Comparable to other walls
  And just as ancient (so they say)
As those they name in history books
  That were not built up in one day!

Built by one man who scorned all help,
  Used neither rubble nor yet sand
To cover up the wall he built—
  That is the pride of Westmorland!

Rex Taylor

A PRAYER FOR THE NEW YEAR

GOD, patient of beginnings,
    Help us this day to see
Time has no real beginning, no real end,
  Just continuity.

Bid us consider gardens;
  Seeds planted in the May,
Then flowers, then frost, then rest, and flowers
    once more.
  And Time yields life this way!

Show us now cause for trusting,
  Who would be fearful when
Years go and come, for life Time bears away,
  Time will bring back again.

Teach us that years, in passing,
  Heal, pardon, make us wise.
Teach us that days, in coming, bring with them
  Fulfillment and surprise.

God, patient of beginnings,
  Help us this day to see
In earthy bulbs, spring flowers; in man, the Christ;
  In years, eternity!

                  Violet Alleyn Storey

JEWELS

I HAVE no need of jewels
  Who, every spring,
Can weave the amethyst of violets
  For a ring.

I have no zest for rubies
  Who can wear
The scarlet of a poppy
  In my hair.

I have no need of gold
  'Mid Midas bloom
Of coltsfoot, marigold and whin
  And blazing broom.

I have no need to fear
  That theft befall;
My bracelets, necklaces and crowns
  Are free to all.

Wendy Wood

"WE THREE KINGS..."

THREE small carollers
  Knocked at the door—
Too shy, when it opened,
  Our alms to implore.

Their lanterns showed faces
  Warm with the light
Of the Star they were singing
  That cold dark night.

" You want some money?
  Why?" . . . They stood dumb ;
Till out shot their secret :
  " A present for Mum."

Three small carollers
  Shone for us then
As true kings of Orient :
  As three wise men.

Gilbert Thomas

GOODNIGHT

SLEEP sweetly in this quiet room
  O thou—whoe'er thou art—
And let no mournful yesterdays
  Disturb thy peaceful heart;
Nor let tomorrow mar thy rest
  With dreams of coming ill.
Thy Maker is thy Changeless Friend:
  His love surrounds thee still.
Forget thyself and all the world,
  Put out each garish light.
The stars are shining overhead—
  Sleep sweetly, then. Good-night!

                                    Anon

ACKNOWLEDGMENTS

To Mr George Ogilvie and Miss Wendy Ogilvie for "In The Woods", "The Shepherd" and "Buttercups" by Will H. Ogilvie: to Sedgwick & Jackson for "Politics" and "Moonlit Apples" by John Drinkwater: to *Punch* for "Homespun" by Helen B. Cruickshank: to the Literary Trustees of Walter de la Mare and the Society of Authors for "Nicholas Nye" and "I Dream Of A Place" by Walter de la Mare: to the Hutchinson Group of Companies for "Firelight," "Homecoming" and "Country Thoughts" by Cecil Roberts and "Westmorland Wall" by Rex Taylor: to Victor Gollancz Ltd for "My Laddie" by Hamish McLaren: to Methuen & Co. Ltd. for "Spring Salmon" by Patrick R. Chalmers: to David & Charles (Holdings) Ltd. for "We Three Kings . . ." by Gilbert Thomas.